Who lived in castles?

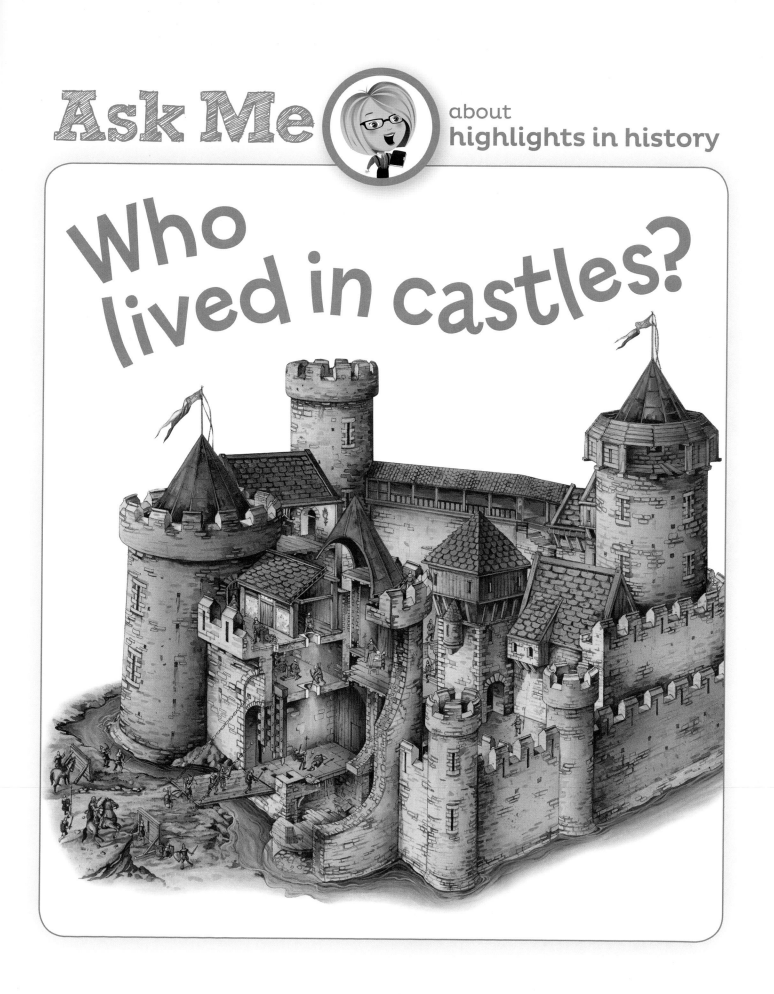

Contents

EAST INDIA TEA CO. BOSTON

18 Who sailed in ice?

20 Who sailed dragon ships?

22 Who made fire dragons?

24 Who were "big-ears"?

26 Who ate boar's head?

28 Who fought the Spanish?

30 Who loved carnivals?

32 Index

What is a time machine?

This book is a kind of time machine! It will take you on a journey back into history. On your journey you will read about things that happened many, many years ago. You will read about castles and knights, kings and queens, pirates, explorers, and inventors. So climb on board—turn the pages, that is—and let's go!

Which king dressed up as the sun?

Louis XIV (the Fourteenth) of France. He became king in 1643, when he was only four years old. Louis chose the sun as his royal symbol, so he was called the Sun King. He enjoyed dancing and dressed up in a sun costume made specially for him.

Who talked to dead kings?

Inca emperors in Peru. An emperor is a kind of leader or ruler, like a king but even more important than a king! About 500 years ago, Peru was ruled by people known as the Inca. When Inca emperors died, their bodies were made into mummies and kept in the palace they had lived in. Once in a while, the mummies were taken from their palaces to the living emperor, who asked the mummies questions about the right time to fight wars or plant crops.

Who lived in castles?

Kings and queens and rich lords and ladies lived in castles in the Middle Ages. The Middle Ages is the name of the time in Europe from around the 400s to the 1400s. The first castles were made of wooden planks, but later ones were built with big stone blocks. Stone castles had thick walls to protect the people inside from enemies.

drawbridge

moat

Fun Facts

In Japan, castles were built with one large tower. This tower was called a tenshu. Gardens, parks, and other buildings surrounded the tenshu. Deep moats protected the castle.

Where was the Wild West?

tower

In the United States. In the 1800s, many people left Britain, Ireland, and other countries in Europe to live in the United States. Some of these settlers rode in wagons to the west of the country. There they fought with Native American tribes and were shot at by robbers, so it became known as the Wild West. Settlers didn't build castles, though. Sometimes the U.S. Army built forts. These forts often had walls, towers, and gates, similar to castles only much smaller.

Who was king of the castles?

King Ludwig II of Bavaria. He loved castles and built several castles and palaces on mountaintops in southern Germany. One of them looked as if it came right out of a fairy tale. Germany is a country in Europe.

Which knights sank?

The German knights who were fighting Russian soldiers on a frozen lake. In 1242, an army of German knights was battling a Russian army on a frozen lake. When the knights moved to a part of the lake where the ice had thinned, it began to crack and the knights sank into the freezing water. Their heavy armor pulled them under the surface.

Fun Facts

Hundreds of years ago soldiers used giant weapons. These included a two-handed sword the height of a man, and pointed sticks called pikes, which were as tall as three people.

8

How many swords make a samurai?

Two. Samurai, fierce knights hundreds of years ago in Japan, always carried two curved swords, one long and one short. They were also good at riding horses and shooting arrows with a bow.

Who fired a duck's foot?

Pirate captains. In the 1700s, a pistol was invented that had four barrels instead of one. The barrel of a pistol is a short tube. It looked like a duck's foot, so that became its name. Sea captains used duck's-foot pistols to make their sailors behave.

NOW YOU KNOW!

In the past, warriors defended themselves and fought with different weapons and armor. Sometimes the armor did more harm than good, though, as when it became too heavy to move in.

Who had a tea party?

The colonists in British North America in 1773. They had to pay money to Britain on goods sent to them from England, such as tea. This payment of money was called a tax. The colonists were unhappy paying taxes they had not voted to accept. One night, they crept on board the British ships in Boston harbor and threw the cargo of tea into the water.

Fun Facts

When the colonists threw the tea overboard, it became known as the Boston Tea Party. The colonists disguised themselves as Mohawk warriors.

Whose flag showed a boot?

Peasants, or poor farm workers, in Germany. In the Middle Ages most flags had designs such as crowns and stars. But when thousands of peasants fought their lords 500 years ago, they designed a new flag. It showed a farmer's muddy boot!

Who else revolted?

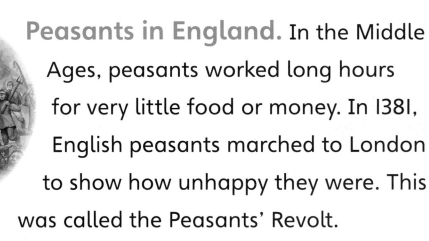

Peasants in England. In the Middle Ages, peasants worked long hours for very little food or money. In 1381, English peasants marched to London to show how unhappy they were. This was called the Peasants' Revolt.

NOW YOU KNOW!

When people don't like how they're treated, they sometimes revolt, or become angry and push back. North American colonists in the 1700s, German peasants in the 1500s, and English peasants in the 1300s all revolted.

Who were highwaymen?

Highwaymen were robbers. In the 1700s, many rich people in Europe traveled in horse-drawn coaches. Highwaymen would stop a coach at gunpoint and demand money and jewels from the travelers inside. Dick Turpin was a famous highwayman who lived in England.

Who hid in a forest?

Robin Hood hid in Sherwood Forest, in England, with his men. Some people believe Robin was an outlaw who lived in the Middle Ages. There are many stories about Robin. Some tell that he stole from the rich and gave to the poor.

Which robber put a bucket on his head?

Ned Kelly, a famous outlaw in Australia. When he was captured by the police, he was wearing a homemade suit of armor. The helmet was shaped like a bucket and was made from a piece of plow.

Fun Facts

In the early 1800s, there were reports of a fierce leader in command of thousands of pirates. Her name was Madame Cheng. Her pirates sailed along the coast of China in the early 1800s in big, wooden sailing ships called junks.

How many people walked the plank?

Maybe one. People once told stories of how pirates punished captives by making them "walk the plank"—into the sea! Pirates were also said to have abandoned (left behind) captives on desert islands. We don't know if pirates really did those things, but they sound like things pirates would do.

Where was the Great Fire?

The Great Fire started in Pudding Lane in London in 1666. Most of London's buildings were made of wood, so the fire spread very quickly. Most of the houses and churches in London burned down. The city was rebuilt using brick and stone instead of wood.

Fun Facts

In 1883, a volcano erupted in Southeast Asia. Most of the island of Krakatoa, near Java, was destroyed.

What disaster was caused by fleas?

The Black Death. In the mid 1300s, millions of people in Europe died in an event known as the Black Death, caused by a disease called plague. Scientists believe people caught the plague when they were bitten by fleas that also had bitten rats sick with the disease. Plague may have started in China. It first came to Europe with rats, and their fleas, that lived on ships sailing between Asia and Europe.

Which city had three disasters?

The city of Lisbon in Portugal. On November 1, 1755, a massive earthquake made the buildings fall down. Then huge waves from the sea flooded the harbor. Finally, the city caught fire.

Who lived on rocks?

Christian men called monks living in Greece a thousand years ago. They put up buildings to live in on top of tall hills of rock. This was because they wanted somewhere quiet to study and pray. Climbing up and down was hard, so the monks climbed into baskets and were raised or lowered with a rope. Only one monk at a time could travel up and down the rock in the basket.

Fun Facts

In 1193, Muslims in Delhi, India, built an amazing tower called the Qutub Minar. It takes 379 stair steps to get to the top of the 238-foot (73-meter) tall tower! The tower is 47 feet (14 meters) across at the bottom, but only 9 feet (3 meters) at the top.

Who wore shell suits and hats?

Pilgrims who had been to Spain. In the Middle Ages, Christians from Europe traveled to Spain to pray to St. James at a special place called a shrine. These pilgrims wore shells, the badge of St. James, on their hats and cloaks to show that they had been to his shrine.

Which temple was covered in gold?

The Golden Temple at Amritsar, in northern India. It was built nearly 500 years ago by Guru Arjan Dev, a leader of the Sikh religion. The walls are made from white marble, and the roofs are covered in gold.

Who sailed in ice?

The explorer Fridtjof Nansen, who jammed his ship into the ice on purpose. Over 100 years ago, Nansen set out to explore the North Pole. Here, thick ice covers the Arctic Ocean and drifts north. Nansen jammed his ship onto the ice so that it would drift north with the ice. Nansen was from Norway. He built a special ship called the *Fram* for his trip to the North Pole in 1893.

Fun Facts

To work out the speed of their ship, explorers sailing on ships used to throw a log attached to a long knotted rope into the sea. The rope was wound up on a reel. The explorers measured how fast they were going by how many "knots" were reeled out in half a minute. This is why the word "knot" is used for the speed of ships.

Who took camels to Australia?

Robert Burke and William Wills in 1860. They took camels with them on an expedition to cross Australia. They shipped 24 camels from India to help carry supplies.

NOW YOU KNOW!

Explorers sometimes used surprising ways to reach unknown areas.

Who sailed dragon ships?

Viking warriors from Scandinavia, in northern Europe.

They sailed along the coasts of western Europe attacking and raiding towns and villages. They would wave axes and swords, set fire to buildings, and steal treasure. They sailed in long ships, with fronts carved to look like monsters or snarling dragons.

When did animals fly in balloons?

In 1783. Two French inventors, Joseph and Jacques Montgolfier, made big balloons for flying. The balloons rose up into the air when a fire heated the air inside them. Their first passengers were a sheep, a duck, and a rooster.

Who flew first?

Orville Wright, an American, in an airplane he and his brother, Wilbur, built. Orville's flight in 1903 was the first of a machine that was heavier than air, powered by a motor, and piloted by a person.

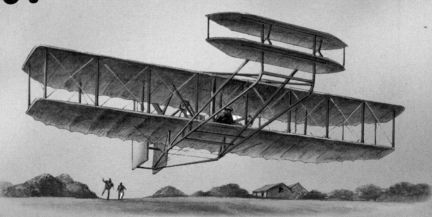

Who made fire dragons?

The Chinese made rockets called "fire dragons" about 1,000 years ago. They used the rockets as weapons in battle. They also called them "flying crows with magic fire." The rockets were filled with gunpowder and lit at the end. The rocket would whoosh straight at the enemy.

NOW YOU KNOW!

Every day, people use things that were invented or discovered hundreds of years ago around the world.

What can see through you?

X-rays, which were discovered in 1895 by German scientist Wilhelm Röntgen. X-rays pass through your skin to take photos of your bones, such as those in your hands, and such organs as your lungs.

Who made mold into medicine?

Alexander Fleming. He discovered that a mold, called Penicillium, could be used as a medicine to kill germs. The medicine was called penicillin. Before penicillin was used, hundreds of people died from infections caused by germs.

Who were "big-ears"?

Some say this was a nickname given to people known as the Inca. In 1532, Spanish soldiers invaded Peru. They had heard the land was rich in gold and wanted to steal it. They saw that every Inca prince and nobleman wore massive earrings made of solid gold. The Spanish are said to have nicknamed the Inca "big-ears."

Who had special nails?

Empress Cixi. More than one hundred years ago, the Chinese Empress Cixi ruled a kingdom in Asia that was not well understood by Westerners. Many stories were told about Cixi. One of them was that she grew her little fingernails until they were 6 inches (15 centimeters) long. Her nails had to be covered by long, gold covers, called shields, to stop the nails from breaking.

24

Who were the fashion leaders?

People in France. France was the center of fashion during the 1860s. In other countries in Europe and in North America, women copied what was being worn in Paris, France's capital city. Most women wore big dresses called hoop skirts.

They were named for their large bell-shaped frames, or hoops, made of steel. Cloth was stretched over the frame to form a skirt.

Fun Facts

The first man to wear a top hat caused quite a stir. In 1800, British hatmaker John Hetherington went out into the streets of London wearing a new style of hat. It was tall, round, and made of shiny silk. People were shocked, and legend has it he was even arrested for disturbing the peace.

Who ate boar's head?

People at a castle feast. In the Middle Ages, lords and ladies held fantastic feasts that might include roast swan or boar's head served on golden plates. Less important people ate off wooden plates or large thick slices of stale bread.

Who used a fork?

No one! In the Middle Ages, people ate with their fingers or knives. Spoons were sometimes used, but forks had not been invented. People began using forks around 1600.

Where did bakers save the city?

In Vienna, Austria, in 1683. Stories are still told of how they were baking bread in the ovens under the shop when they heard a strange sound. Turkish invaders were trying to dig a tunnel under the city walls! The bakers raised the alarm, and the city was saved.

Fun Facts

Flavored water ice was a popular treat hundreds of years ago. Tales are told of a wedding at which 34 flavors were served.

Who fought the Spanish?

Sir Francis Drake, one of the best sea captains in England. In 1588, a huge fleet of Spanish warships, called the Armada, set sail to attack England. Sir Francis Drake was ordered to meet them and fight them off. According to English legend, he was in Plymouth playing a game of bowls, and he wanted to finish his game before joining the battle. He still defeated the Spanish.

Fun Facts

About 500 years ago, a Native American tribe called the Iroquois played a ball game called baggataway. Hundreds of people played the game at the same time.

Who played board games?

People in India, a thousand years ago. Players started in the center of the board and had to move their counters north, south, east, and west before heading home. Shells were thrown instead of dice. The game was called pachisi. Today a similar board game is still played: parcheesi.

Who was given a silver tennis ball?

In the Middle Ages, champions at a game much like today's tennis were rewarded with a ball made of silver.

The game was still popular in the 1700s, when one French player used to show off by jumping in and out of a barrel between shots!

Who loved carnivals?

The Venetians, people of the city of Venice.

Starting in the Middle Ages, many countries held carnivals, but the best carnival was in Venice, Italy. People wore fantastic costumes and danced in the streets all night. They also wore masks so that they would not be recognized if they were naughty!

Fun Facts

Every summer, children in Dinkelsbühl, Germany, have a street parade. They remember how a girl helped to save the town by leading all the children out to meet the Swedish army when it attacked. The army felt sorry for them and stopped its attack.

Who celebrates the sun god?

People in Peru. Thousands celebrate the festival of Inti Raymi, which takes place in June. Originally held for the sun god, there is lots of drumming and dancing.

Whose plot exploded?

Guy Fawkes. He tried (but failed) to blow up the Houses of Parliament, a government building, in London, England, in 1605. Every year on November 5, there are fireworks parties to remember him.

Index

© 2013 Southwestern Advantage
Nashville, Tennessee
ISBN 978-0-87197-582-9

Originally published as *Ask Me*
Southwestern/Great American, Inc.
© 2002, 2005, 2010, 2011, 2012
Southwestern Advantage
Nashville, Tennessee
ISBN 0-87197-519-X
www.southwesternadvantage.com

Printed by RR Donnelley, Shenzhen, Guangdong, China

Henry Bedford
*Chief Executive Officer, Southwestern/
Great American, Inc.*

Dan Moore
President, Southwestern Advantage

Editorial Director
Mary Cummings

Managing Editor
Judy Jackson

Senior Editor
Barbara J. Reed

Production Manager
Powell Ropp

Senior Art Directors
Steve Newman
Starletta Polster

Senior Designer
Travis Rader

Composition and Production Design
Sara Anglin
Jessie Anglin

The publishers would like to thank the following artists whose work appears in this book: Barbara Ball, John Butler, Steve Caldwell, Jim Channell, Kuo Kang Chen, Andrew Clark, Mark Davis, Peter Dennis, Heather Dickinson, Richard Draper, James Field, Nicholas Forder, Chris Forsey, Mike Foster/Maltings Partnership, Terry Gabbey, Alan Hancocks, Richard Hook, John James, Emma Jones, Tony Kenyon, Aziz Khan, Sue King/SGA, Kevin Maddison, Janos Marffy, Debbie Meekcoms, Helen Parsley, Rachel Philips, Jane Pickering, Neil Reid, Terry Riley, Pete Roberts, Steve Roberts, Martin Sanders, Peter Sarson, Mike Saunders, Sarah Smith, Studio Galante, Rudi Vizi, Mike White, Peter Wilks, Paul Williams.

Images/art © Thinkstock:
Dinosaurs and Prehistoric Animals: page 25
Highlights in History: pages 7, 9
Reptiles and Birds: page 9
Science: pages 11, 30

Images © NASA
Space: pages 10, 11, 24